W9-CEN-401

Poptropica

MYTHOLOGY

by Tracey West

Poptropica
An Imprint of Penguin Group (USA) Inc.

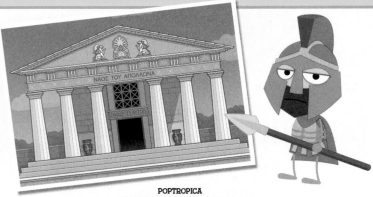

POPTROPICA
Published by the Penguin Group
Penguin Group (USA) Inc., 375 Hudson Street, New York, New York 10014, USA

USA | Canada | UK | Ireland | Australia | New Zealand | India | South Africa | China
Penguin Books Ltd, Registered Offices: 80 Strand, London WC2R ORL, England

For more information about the Penguin Group visit penguin.com

All rights reserved. No part of this book may be reproduced, scanned, or distributed in any
printed or electronic form without permission. Please do not participate in or encourage piracy of
copyrighted materials in violation of the author's rights. Purchase only authorized editions.

The publisher does not have any control over and does not assume any
responsibility for author or third-party websites or their content.

Photo credits: cover: © iStockphoto/Thinkstock; page 5: © iStockphoto/Thinkstock; page 6: © Hemera/
Thinkstock; page 8: © iStockphoto.com/gioadventures; page 10: © Photos.com/Getty Images/Thinkstock;
page 12: © iStockphoto.com/GeorgiosArt; page 13: © iStockphoto/Thinkstock; page 14: © iStockphoto/
Thinkstock; page 16: © iStockphoto/Thinkstock; page 17: © iStockphoto/Thinkstock; page 18: © iStockphoto/
Thinkstock; page 22: © Hemera/Thinkstock; page 24: © Hemera/Thinkstock; page 26: © iStockphoto/
Thinkstock; page 32: (illustration of the Pleiades) © Dorling Kindersley RF/Thinkstock, (ancient Greek
amphora) © iStockphoto/Thinkstock; page 33: © iStockphoto/Thinkstock; page 34: © Hemera/Thinkstock;
page 35: (Doric column) © Hemera/Thinkstock, (Ionic column) © iStockphoto/Thinkstock, (Corinthian
column) © iStockphoto/Thinkstock; page 38: © iStockphoto/Thinkstock; page 39: © iStockphoto/
Thinkstock; page 42: (vase depicting Odysseus) © Photos.com/Getty Images/Thinkstock, (stamp of Odysseus
and Sirens) © iStockphoto/Thinkstock; page 43: © iStockphoto/Thinkstock; page 44: © iStockphoto/
Thinkstock; page 45: © Photos.com/Getty Images/Thinkstock; page 46: © iStockphoto/Thinkstock; page
47: © iStockphoto/Thinkstock; page 48: (Greek vase) © Hemera/Thinkstock, (illustration of a Minotaur)
iStockphoto.com/duncan1890; page 52: (graphic icon of Perseus) © iStockphoto/Thinkstock; (sculpture
of arm holding Medusa's head) © Hemera/Thinkstock, (bronze statue of Perseus holding Medusa's head)
© iStockphoto/Thinkstock; page 54: © iStockphoto/Thinkstock; page 55: © iStockphoto/Thinkstock;
page 56: © (illustration of Hercules wrestling the Hydra) iStockphoto/Thinkstock, (sculpture of Hercules)
iStockphoto/Thinkstock; page 57: © iStockphoto.com/yaxxcom; page 58: © Hemera/Thinkstock.

© 2007-2013 Pearson Education, Inc. All rights reserved. Published by Poptropica, an imprint of
Penguin Group (USA) Inc., 345 Hudson Street, New York, New York 10014. Printed in the U.S.A.

ISBN 978-0-448-47793-0   1 0 9 8 7 6 5 4 3 2

ALWAYS LEARNING   PEARSON

Poptopics: Connecting Poptropica to the Real World

The Islands of Poptropica are definitely fantastic, but they're all grounded in reality. Every time and place you visit there is somehow connected to the real world.

This book takes a real-world look at **Mythology Island**. Everything you experience in Mythology Island is connected to the culture and myths of ancient Greece—and here you'll learn the stories behind them all.

Look for this symbol to see examples of how classical Greek culture has survived into modern times. **POP CULTURE**

This symbol will alert you to amazing facts about Greek culture. **POP FACTS**

Welcome to Ancient Greece!

If you visit Poptropica's Mythology Island, you'll find that it resembles the classical period of ancient Greece. This period took place between about 500 BCE and 323 BCE. It was an exciting time in history. The city of Athens experimented with democracy. Great philosophers introduced ideas that would change the world. Playwrights produced works of literature that have stood the test of time, and artists created amazing statues and objects.

Meet the Immortals

On Mythology Island, you'll encounter several Greek gods and goddesses on your adventure. Classical Greeks worshipped these immortals and told stories about them. Today, a few thousand years later, their legends live on in books, TV shows, and films.

The gods and goddesses on the Island include the immortals known as the twelve Olympians, the major gods of the Greeks. You'll also meet some other immortals, including Hades (who's a major god but doesn't live on Mount Olympus) and Triton, who's the son of a god.

The Twelve Olympians

Zeus

Poseidon

Athena

Apollo

Aphrodite

Hephaestus

Artemis

Hermes

Hera

Demeter

Ares

Dionysus

Zeus

Hades

Poseidon

When in Rome . . . Do as the Greeks Do

The ancient Roman and Greek civilizations were similar in many ways. The ancient Romans matched up their gods and goddesses to the Greek immortals. So there is a corresponding Roman god or goddess with a Latin name for each Greek one.

Mount Olympus, Home of the Gods

Mount Olympus is a real mountain in Greece. At 9,570 feet high, it's the tallest in the country. It sits on the eastern side of Greece, near the Aegean Sea.

In ancient times, people believed that Mount Olympus was home to the gods and goddesses they worshipped. Maybe they could imagine the immortals looking down on them from high atop the mountain.

Life on Olympus

Thomas Bulfinch was a bank clerk who lived in the 1800s and researched world mythology in his spare time. In his famous book *Bulfinch's Mythology*, he describes how the gods and goddesses lived in their heavenly abode:

- A gate of clouds opened to allow the immortals into their home.
- Poseidon and Hades would leave their realms to join the other gods in great feasts.
- They ate delicious food called ambrosia and drank nectar.
- Apollo entertained them by playing his lyre, backed up by the Muses.

POP CULTURE

In the twentieth century, American cooks created "ambrosia" salad intended to resemble the food of the gods. It usually contains whipped cream, marshmallows, canned fruit, and coconut. Does that sound heavenly to you?

Snow or No?

The peaks of Mount Olympus are snowcapped, and often covered with clouds. But the ancient Greek poet Homer wrote this about Mount Olympus: "Neither is it shaken by winds nor ever wet with rain, nor does snow fall upon it, but the air is outspread clear and cloudless, and over it hovers a radiant whiteness." Some scholars think that Homer meant that the mountain's top peak, where the gods lived, rose above the clouds and the snow. Or he might have just been being poetic.

Zeus

His Head Is in the Clouds

Zeus was the son of Cronus, king of the Titans. Cronus heard a prophecy that one of his children would one day dethrone him, so he swallowed them all after they were born. Zeus's mother, Rhea, got smart when Zeus was born. She wrapped a stone in a blanket and Cronus swallowed that instead. When Zeus grew up, he defeated his father in battle and forced him to vomit up the children he'd eaten. After he banished the Titans, Zeus and his brothers and sisters became the gods and goddesses of Olympus.

Zeus became known as king of the gods as well as the humans. He ruled from Mount Olympus, and in his spare time he created storms and controlled the weather—and meddled in the lives of humans.

ZEUS

ROMAN NAME: JUPITER OR JOVE
GOD OF: THE SKY, WEATHER
ALSO KNOWN AS: KING OF THE GODS
SYMBOLS: THUNDERBOLT, EAGLE
MARRIED TO: HERA

God of Thunder

Some ancient works of art show Zeus wielding a thunderbolt as a weapon. He's also always shown with a beard, but that's just for looks.

If you ever watch an old black-and-white movie, you might hear someone say, "By Jove!" It's an exclamation of surprise that references the Roman ruler of the gods.

POP CULTURE

Poseidon

Kind of Like Aquaman, but More Powerful

When the Titans fell, Poseidon gained control of the oceans and other waters. He lived under the sea in a golden palace, where he controlled the ocean waves and communicated with sea creatures.

The Greeks also worshipped Poseidon as a bringer of earthquakes and a god of horses. The Romans rejected this land connection and kept their version of Poseidon, Neptune, in the water.

POSEIDON

ROMAN NAME: NEPTUNE
GOD OF: THE SEA, EARTHQUAKES, AND HORSES
SYMBOL: TRIDENT, DOLPHIN, TUNA

The Trident

Poseidon is usually shown carrying this three-pronged spear. Some think it may have once been a kind of fishing spear, but it also makes a pretty cool weapon—and it is what he used to create earthquakes.

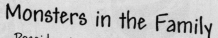

Monsters in the Family

Poseidon is credited with having many children—some human, and some monsters. These included Polyphemus, a one-eyed Cyclops, and Antaeus, a giant. In Mythology Island, his son Triton appears as a blue-skinned surfer dude. In Greek myths, however, he's a merman with the tail of a fish. He carries a seashell with him that can calm or raise the ocean waves when he blows into it.

You can find King Triton in Disney's *The Little Mermaid*, and King Neptune is an occasional guest on *SpongeBob SquarePants*.

POP CULTURE

Hades

Zombies Would Probably Dig Him

When Hades and his brothers drew straws to see which kingdom they would get to rule, he probably got the worst deal. Hades went below the earth to rule the Underworld—the land of the dead.

Hades didn't punish the souls that were sent to live with him for eternity. He left that task to the Furies. These three sisters are often pictured with wings. They were cruel when they doled out punishment, but they made sure that the recipient truly deserved it.

All that sunlight deprivation may have affected Hades's mood, because he's often portrayed as stern and without pity.

HADES

ROMAN NAME: PLUTO
GOD OF: THE UNDERWORLD
COOL HAT: HELMET OF INVISIBILITY
MARRIED TO: PERSEPHONE

You Can't See Me!

Hades owned a special helmet that made him invisible when he wore it. Legend says that a Cyclops gave it to him during the battle against the Titans. The name Hades also means "unseen" or "invisible."

Staff of Death

Hades is often shown carrying a scepter, a staff held by a ruler that basically indicates he's the guy in charge. Some artists like to show skulls carved into the scepter. Wicked!

The name Pluto is also shared by a dwarf planet in our solar system, and Mickey Mouse's dog.

POP CULTURE

The Underworld

People Are Dying to Get In

When you hear *Underworld*, you might think it was a dark and scary place. But it wasn't all bad. Once you entered the Underworld, you were judged on whether or not you were a good person in life. Then you were sent to one of three levels:

- The Elysian Fields: This beautiful paradise was reserved for only the most righteous people, or those blessed by the gods. Kind of like an eternal party.
- The Plain of Asphodel: This middle level was nothing special. If you were a regular and not especially good person, you'd end up here, floating around like a ghost. Boring, but at least it wasn't horrible.

- Tartarus: The lowest level of Hades is where the really bad people got sent to be tormented by the Furies. No fun at all.

Ferryman of the Dead

Ancient Greeks believed that when they died, the god Hermes took them to the banks of one of the rivers bordering the Underworld. There they would meet a man rowing a boat who would take them across the river. His name was Charon, and in art he was originally pictured as an old man. Charon charged one coin for the trip, and those who didn't have it had to wait on the banks of the river for a hundred years. That's why ancient Greeks placed a coin in the mouth of a dead body before it was buried.

Athena

She'll Win the War— and Then Weave a Wicked Rug

Athena's main role was as a protector of the ancient Greeks, and so she became known as a goddess of war. Unlike Ares, the god of war, she was known more for skill and strategy in battle than for stuff like blood and violence. When she was born, she burst from Zeus's forehead wearing armor, and it's usually how she's portrayed in works of art.

The fact that she came from a forehead connects to Athena's other role as a goddess of wisdom—she was very smart. She also became known as a goddess of crafts, especially spinning and weaving.

ATHENA

ROMAN NAME: MINERVA
ALSO KNOWN AS: PALLAS
GODDESS OF: WAR, WISDOM, CRAFTS
SYMBOLS: OLIVE TREE, OWL, SNAKE
COOL ACCESSORY: THE AEGIS

Battle Swag

When Athena went into battle, she wore an aegis—a leather shield with golden tassels hanging from it that protected her from harm. It used to belong to her father, Zeus. Many images show the aegis emblazoned with a picture of the Gorgon Medusa's head (see page 46 for her story), because Athena was the one who turned Medusa's hair into snakes.

Athena and Arachne

Arachne was a poor, motherless girl who became known for her amazing weaving skills. People said, "You must have been taught by Athena herself!" But Arachne denied it; she had taught herself and was proud of it.

When Athena heard that, she disguised herself as an old woman and approached Arachne. She told Arachne that if she asked the goddess for forgiveness, she would get it, but Arachne refused.

Poof! Athena transformed back into a goddess and challenged Arachne to a weaving contest. They both wove something amazing, and Athena couldn't find anything wrong with what Arachne created. That made her angry, so she turned Arachne into a spider so she could weave for all eternity. (And that, by the way, is why spiders are known as *arachnids*.)

POP FACTS

In many myths, all the immortals of Mount Olympus are shown to be very jealous and vindictive—not just Athena.

Battle of the Immortals: Poseidon vs. Athena!

The details of this legend vary, but it seems to have gone down something like this:

- Poseidon and Athena both had their eyes on a city that didn't have a patron god or goddess. They decided to have a contest: Whoever could provide the city with the greatest gift would claim it.
- Poseidon stuck his trident into the ground and water sprang up—salt water, which flooded and became a sea.

- Athena stuck her spear into the ground and planted the first olive tree.
- The judges of the contest (probably Zeus and the other gods of Mount Olympus) gave the win to Athena. They thought that the olive tree was a pretty useful gift because it provided food, fuel, and wood.
- The city was named Athens and the olive tree became a symbol of Athena.

PICK ★ ONE ★ NOW!!!

Winner: Athena!

Apollo

He's a God of Many Faces, and They're All Handsome

Young, handsome, and with a personality as bright as the sun—it's no wonder Apollo was one of the most popular gods. It wasn't always this way; early myths show him as a superpowerful, punishing god who was feared by the other immortals. But he became more well-known as a god of the arts, transforming him into sort of the rock star of Mount Olympus. Out in the country, people who took care of sheep and goats worshipped him as their protector.

Apollo's mother was Leto, a Titan, and his twin sister was Artemis, the goddess of the hunt. Both twins were known as being experts with a bow and arrow.

APOLLO

ROMAN NAME: APOLLO (YES, IT'S THE SAME)
ALSO KNOWN AS: PHOEBUS
GOD OF: MUSIC, POETRY, DANCE, PROPHECY,
   HEALING, SHEPHERDS, HERDSMEN
SYMBOLS: LYRE, RAVEN, BOW AND ARROW
TWIN SISTER: ARTEMIS

POP
CULTURE

The Apollo Theater in New York City's Harlem neighborhood has hosted some of the greatest African American musical performers in the world.

Into the Future . . .

Apollo's temple was located in the ancient town of Delphi, which was supposed to be the center of the world. It was guarded by a huge serpent or dragon called Python, and Apollo slew the dragon with his bow and arrow and claimed the city for himself.

Visitors to Apollo's temple would come with questions they wanted the god to answer for them. Their questions would be given to a female priest called the Pythia (named after the dragon). They believed that the Pythia could give them an answer from Apollo, or even tell them the future. Other gods and temples had oracles, but Apollo's oracle at Delphi was the most famous.

The Muses

Apollo's Back-Up Singers

Although they weren't always connected to Apollo, these nine goddesses of the arts became a natural fit with the handsome god of song. That's why you'll find them in Apollo's temple in Poptropica's Mythology Island.

Some stories say there were three Muses, but the ancient poet Hesiod named nine of them, and these are the nine that became popular. Each Muse came to be known as the patron of a different aspect of the arts.

CALLIOPE: MUSE OF EPIC POETRY

CLIO: MUSE OF HISTORY

ERATO: MUSE OF LOVE POETRY

The word *museum* comes from a Greek word meaning "a shrine to the Muses."

POP CULTURE

EUTERPE: MUSE OF MUSIC (ESPECIALLY FLUTES)

MELPOMENE: MUSE OF TRAGEDY

POLYHYMNIA: MUSE OF SACRED POETRY

TERPSICHORE: MUSE OF DANCING AND CHORAL SONG

THALIA: MUSE OF COMEDY

URANIA: MUSE OF ASTRONOMY

POP FACTS

In ancient Greece, poetry and music were connected because early poets were also musicians who played music to accompany the poetry they read.

Aphrodite

More Than Just a Pretty Face

Known for her stunning beauty, Aphrodite is usually called the goddess of love. With magic, she could make gods fall in love with mortals, or mortals fall in love with gods, or mortals fall in love with mortals, or . . . you get the idea. She created more problems than the writer of a soap opera.

She wasn't all trouble. She was very kind and helpful to her favorite mortals. Animals loved her, and birds like the dove and sparrow pulled her chariot. The poet Homer said that her parents were Zeus and the Titan Dione, but the poet Hesiod said she was born from the foam of the ocean waves. That might be one reason she is considered a goddess of the sea.

ROMAN NAME: VENUS

ALSO KNOWN AS: KYPRIS OR LADY
   OF CYPRUS

GODDESS OF: LOVE, BEAUTY, FERTILITY

SYMBOLS: DOVE, APPLE, SCALLOP
   SHELL, MIRROR

MARRIED TO: HEPHAESTUS

The Men in Her Life

Aphrodite was married to Hephaestus, the god of fire and metalworking. Those are pretty cool things to be a god of, but Hephaestus was ugly and couldn't walk, and some say Zeus made Aphrodite marry him.

Aphrodite's son Eros, the god of love, had Ares as a father. Known as Cupid by the Romans, Eros carried a bow and arrow, and if he shot you with it, you would fall in love with the next person you saw.

So those little winged cherubs on Valentine's Day cards? They're based on Eros, the god of love.

POP CULTURE

Artemis

She's Young, Wild, and Free

Her twin brother, Apollo, shone like the sun, but Artemis
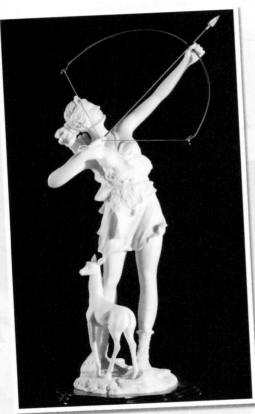
was more of a moon girl.
You might have found
her dancing in the shady
forest with tree spirits
called nymphs.

Artemis was the
protector of wild animals
but also the goddess
of hunting. This might
seem like a conflict, but
her job was to protect
the young animals until
they were old enough to
hunt. In ancient times,
people needed to hunt
to survive, so Artemis
played an important
role.

Images of Artemis
usually show her with
a bow and arrow, a
stag, or a hunting dog. She is most often
portrayed as a girl or young woman.

ARTEMIS

ROMAN NAME: DIANA
GODDESS OF: WILD ANIMALS, HUNTING, CHILDBIRTH
SYMBOLS: CYPRESS TREE
TWIN BROTHER: APOLLO

Awesome Poetry

The Homeric Hymns are a collection of poems dedicated to the gods and goddesses that might have been written by Homer, but no one is sure. This is from a hymn to Artemis:

"Over the shadowy hills and windy peaks she draws her golden bow. . . . The tops of the high mountains tremble and the tangled wood echoes awesomely with the outcry of beasts."

Why was Artemis a goddess of childbirth? Because right after she was born, she helped her mother deliver her twin brother, Apollo.

POP FACTS

Nice Trick!

Once, two giants decided to attack Mount Olympus. Artemis tricked them by turning into a deer and running between them. They both went after the deer—and ended up spearing each other.

25

Hermes

He Might Have Invented Multitasking

If Hermes were around today, he would be the guy with the latest version of every phone and device. The son of Zeus and a Titan's daughter named Maia, he was all about connecting gods to men, and men to gods.

As messenger of the gods, he wore winged sandals to get him where he needed to go faster than a 4G connection. Because he traveled everywhere, he became a god of roads and also diplomacy—the skill of communicating with strangers and keeping things friendly.

There isn't enough room on this page to talk about all the things that Hermes was god of. In his spare time, he invented things like the alphabet, numbers, and gymnastics. He was a busy god—which might be why he doesn't make an appearance in Mythology Island.

HERMES

ROMAN NAME: MERCURY

GOD OF: ROADS, MESSENGERS, DIPLOMACY, THIEVES, WRITING, GYMNASTICS (AND A LOT OF OTHER STUFF)

JOBS: MESSENGER OF THE GODS; BRINGS THE DEAD TO THE UNDERWORLD

SYMBOLS: CADUCEUS, WINGED SANDALS

A Misunderstood Symbol

The staff Hermes carried is best known as a caduceus. The wings at the top symbolize his speed, and the intertwined snakes symbolize peace, because they're not fighting each other. The staff was like a magic wand that could do things such as open locked doors or put people to sleep. Asclepius, the god of healing, carried a staff with one snake wrapped around it, but it's the caduceus that went on to become a symbol of medicine and of the US Army Medical Corps. The caduceus is really a symbol of magic.

Much More Than a Jealous Wife

People worshipped Hera as a goddess of the sky and the stars. Maybe that's why she was married to Zeus, the ruler of the sky. Hera is portrayed as a beautiful queen who sits on a golden throne, wearing a jeweled crown.

Hera and Zeus might seem like a match made in heaven. Hera was wise, and Zeus sought her advice a lot. But mostly Zeus cheated on her, and they argued a lot and found creative ways to get revenge on each other. Even so, she was an important goddess to women. They called on her for help during childbirth, like they did with Artemis.

HERA

ROMAN NAME: JUNO
GODDESS OF: MARRIAGE, THE SKY
JOB: QUEEN OF THE GODS
SYMBOLS: CROWN, SCEPTER, PEACOCK
MARRIED TO: ZEUS

Demeter

She Makes Things Grow

As goddess of agriculture and grains, Demeter was important to ancient people who relied on a good harvest every year for their survival. She is often portrayed wearing a garland around her head made of ears of corn, and carrying a basket filled with fruit, flowers, and grain.

One of the most enduring Greek myths involves Demeter and her daughter, Persephone. Hades pulled Persephone into the Underworld against her will to become his wife. Demeter searched the earth for her, and while she did, no crops grew. Her brother Zeus told Hades that he had to give Persephone back to her mother, but Persephone had already eaten from a pomegranate, which tied her to the Underworld. Persephone was allowed back into the world during spring and summer, when a happy Demeter allowed crops to grow. But when Persephone returned to the Underworld every fall and winter, nothing grew.

DEMETER

ROMAN NAME: CERES
GODDESS OF: GRAINS, FARMING,
   THE HARVEST
MOTHER OF: PERSEPHONE

Ares

He'd Probably Love Today's Video Games

The god of war, Ares was probably the least popular of the gods on Mount Olympus. It might have something to do with his personality. His half sister Athena was a war goddess, but she was mostly concerned with battle strategy and protecting people during wars. Ares, on the other hand, loved all the bad stuff about war: blood, death, and destruction.

ARES

ROMAN NAME: MARS
GOD OF: WAR

Twisted Sister

Ares had a sister named Eris, who was a goddess of conflict. She loved to cause trouble and was best known for starting the Trojan War. Upset about not being invited to a wedding, Eris threw a golden apple into the crowd that was inscribed "To the fairest." Hera, Athena, and Aphrodite each claimed it. Zeus ordered a mortal Trojan named Paris to decide who was the "fairest." Paris chose Aphrodite, who awarded him the beautiful Helen of Troy. However, Helen's husband wasn't happy with this arrangement and led an army of Greek soldiers to Troy to get her back.

Dionysus

Don't Worry, Be Happy

Ancient Greeks liked Dionysus a lot more than they liked his half brother Ares. Ares was all about fighting, but Dionysus was all about having a good time. People connected him to festivities, the discovery of grapes and wine, and all the pleasures found in nature. He's usually portrayed as either a bearded older man or a younger guy with long hair.

DIONYSUS

ROMAN NAME: LIBER
ALSO KNOWN AS: BACCHUS
GOD OF: WINE, FRUITFULNESS, FUN
FRIENDS: SATYRS, NYMPHS

Wild Thing

In Mythology Island, you'll meet a guy with a bushy beard and horns called a satyr. A satyr was a spirit of the wilderness who had some animal as well as human features. Satyrs liked to hang out with Dionysus. The satyr in Poptropica resembles Pan, the god of herdsmen. Besides horns, he had the legs and tail of a goat and played pipes made from reeds.

In Fashion: The Chiton

A popular garment in classical Greece was the chiton. Both men and women wore this simple garment. It was made by taking two long rectangular pieces of fabric and sewing down the sides and across the top, leaving openings for the head and arms. Most men and children wore knee-length

chitons, but a woman's chiton always reached her ankles. Like the Poptropicans of Mythology Island, some Greeks wore a piece of fabric draped over their chiton, called a himation.

You might be wondering: Why didn't they wear togas? A toga was a big piece of fabric that was draped around the body in a very specific way, and could only be worn by citizens of Rome (not Greece).

Painted Pottery

Some of the most impressive art that archaeologists have dug up from classical Greek times is painted pottery. First, one artist would create a vessel out of clay, and then usually turn it over to another artist to be painted. The paintings showed people, animals, and elaborate geometric designs. Many painters depicted scenes from Greek mythology.

What's for Dinner?

Citizens of
Mythology Island
can grab a bite
to eat at a fast-
food restaurant owned by Hercules. Back in ancient Greece,
wealthy people had slaves who cooked for them. The poorer
classes cooked their own food or bought it from street
vendors who sold items like small fried fish (but probably
not Herc's fish nuggets). They also went out for drinks and
snacks in taverns that people ran out of their homes.

Artichokes, carrots, figs, grapes, apples,
chickpeas, fish, squid, chicken, goat,
barley, wheat, and honey are just some of
the foods found in both the ancient and
current Greek diet.

POP FACTS

Amazing Temples

Classical Greek temples and other important buildings feature stone columns set into a stone foundation. One of the greatest temples in ancient Athens was the Parthenon, which still stands today. The fifty outer columns are made of white marble. It was built to honor the goddess Athena, and used to contain a forty-foot-tall statue of her made of gold and ivory.

THE PARTHENON IS 101.34 FEET WIDE AND 228.14 FEET LONG, AND WAS BUILT USING 13,400 STONES.

Can't get to Greece? Then head to Nashville, Tennessee, to see a life-size replica of the Parthenon It contains the city's art museum.

POP CULTURE

Three Columns

There are three main types of columns in classical Greek architecture:

DORIC
STURDY AND PLAIN

IONIC
CURLED ON TOP

CORINTHIAN
SUPERFANCY

POP CULTURE

If you've ever toured Washington, DC, then you've probably seen Greek columns. There are Doric-style columns on the Lincoln Memorial, Ionic-style columns on the Jefferson Memorial, and Corinthian-style columns on the Supreme Court building.

Meet the Monsters

The stories of Greek mythology are just loaded with monsters. Epic tales tell stories of gods and human heroes alike facing all kinds of dangerous, disgusting, and magical beasts. Some of them are humans who were cursed by the gods and turned into monsters. Many of them like to eat people.

They may sound terrible, but look at it this way—without monsters, heroes would have nothing to do.

POP FACTS

A collection of stories and pictures of monsters is called a bestiary.

CERBERUS

The Sphinx

You Don't Want to Fail Her Pop Quiz

- ☐ LION'S BODY
- ☐ WOMAN'S HEAD
- ☐ EAGLE'S WINGS
- ☐ SNAKE'S TAIL

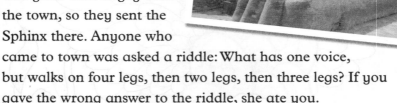

Myths about the Sphinx can be found in both ancient Egypt and Greece. The most famous comes from the Greek town of Thebes. The gods were angry with the town, so they sent the Sphinx there. Anyone who came to town was asked a riddle: What has one voice, but walks on four legs, then two legs, then three legs? If you gave the wrong answer to the riddle, she ate you.

Then along came a guy named Oedipus. He knew the answer to the riddle: a human, who crawls on four legs as a baby, walks on two legs as an adult, and leans on a cane when old. Knowing she was defeated, the Sphinx threw herself off a mountain, and Thebes was saved.

In Mythology Island, you won't have to answer a riddle, but the Sphinx will have a special challenge for you.

Cerberus

He Doesn't Just Play Dead—He Plays *with* the Dead

- ❏ THREE HEADS
- ❏ LION'S CLAWS
- ❏ SNAKE'S TAIL
- ❏ SNAKE'S HEADS DOWN HIS BACK

The poet Hesiod wrote that Cerberus had *fifty* heads!

POP FACTS

Cerberus was the guard dog of the Underworld. He kept the dead from leaving once they entered—some accounts say that he would eat anyone who tried to escape!

In Poptropica's Mythology Island, you'll be charged with getting a whisker from Cerberus. Hercules had a more difficult task—he was asked to carry Cerberus out of the Underworld. Persephone, the wife of Hades, helped him succeed. The legends don't say how, but we can guess that Persephone had a way to tame the savage beast.

The Hydra

Because Nine Heads Are Better Than One

- ☐ GIGANTIC
- ☐ NINE HEADS
- ☐ WHEN ONE HEAD IS CUT OFF,
  TWO MORE GROW BACK

POP FACTS

The Hydra is most often described as having nine heads. The Hydra in Mythology Island has five.

Warning: Gross!

The most famous story of the Hydra takes place in a town called Lerna. The Hydra lived in the swampy waters there. Getting rid of the Hydra was one of the twelve labors given to Hercules (more on these labors later in the book), so he and his nephew Iolaus went to Lerna to do the job.

Hercules had no trouble slicing off the Hydra's heads. The problem was, when he cut

off one head, two would grow back in its place. To solve that problem, Hercules had Iolaus place a burning branch over the wound each time he severed a head, sealing it.

Not satisfied with just killing it, Hercules buried one head under a rock. He dipped his arrows into poison venom from the head, which sounded like a good idea, until his wife accidentally killed him with the poison years later. So in the end, the battle of Hercules vs. the Hydra ended in a tie.

The Sirens

Easily Defeated with Earplugs

- ❏ BODY OF A BIRD
- ❏ HEAD OF A WOMAN
- ❏ ENCHANTS YOU WITH A SONG

The Greek hero Odysseus and his crew encountered three Sirens as they sailed past the Sirens' island in the waters of the Mediterranean. Luckily, the sorceress Circe had warned him about the Sirens. They sang a song that would enchant the sailors, causing them to crash into the rocks. To avoid this, Odysseus had his crew stuff their ears with wax. Then he made them tie him to the mast of the ship so he could listen to the song himself.

There are a few myths that explain the origin of the Sirens. One says that they were three maidens who were Persephone's best friends. After she was kidnapped, Demeter gave them the bodies of birds so that they could fly over the earth, searching for their lost friend.

The Cyclopes

Maybe They Get a Discount on Eyeglasses

- ❏ REALLY BIG
- ❏ ONE SINGLE EYE IN THE CENTER OF FOREHEAD
- ❏ EATS PEOPLE

Warning: Gross!

The Cyclopes (plural of Cyclops, in case you're wondering) were a race of giants who lived on an island. Each Cyclops had one eye, and they mostly ate goats and sheep unless some tasty humans came ashore.

The biggest and most famous Cyclops is Polyphemus, the son of Poseidon. When the Greek hero Odysseus came to the island, he and his men were trapped in Polyphemus's cave. The Cyclops ate some sailors, and then he asked Odysseus his name. Odysseus replied, "Nobody," and Polyphemus chuckled. He said he would eat Nobody last.

But Odysseus got him to drink a bunch of wine, and Polyphemus fell asleep. Then Odysseus blinded the Cyclops's one eye with a flaming torch. When Polyphemus cried out for help, the other Cyclopes asked who was after him. "Nobody!" the giant cried, and Odysseus escaped.

Centaurs

You Don't Want to Horse Around with These Guys

- ❑ UPPER BODY OF A HUMAN
- ❑ LEGS AND LOWER BODY OF A HORSE

These half-man, half-horse creatures were said to live in caves in the mountains of the Greek region of Thessaly. Wild and savage, they had a reputation for causing a lot of trouble. They fought using stones and branches as weapons.

The most famous centaur, however, wasn't violent at all. His name was Chiron, and he was known for his wisdom and skills in medicine. He gave advice to many Greek heroes, including Hercules.

Harpies

They Did Zeus's Dirty Work for Him

- ❏ HUMAN BODY
- ❏ WINGS
- ❏ SOMETIMES DESCRIBED AS HAVING HIDEOUS FACES AND SHARP CLAWS
- ❏ BAD SMELL

The first stories of the Harpies described them as spirits of the wind. The word *harpies* comes from a Greek word meaning "swift robbers," and it was thought that Zeus used the Harpies to scoop up people from earth and bring them to the clouds.

In later stories about the Harpies, they're a lot scarier, with ugly faces and supersharp claws. These are the Harpies that Zeus sent after a blind king named Phineas. He had the Harpies swipe every plate of food put down in front of him, and anything left reeked of the Harpies' terrible stench. Phineas asked for help from a band of heroes known as the Argonauts, and they got rid of the Harpies for him.

Medusa Was the Pretty One

- ❏ HAIR OF SNAKES
- ❏ WINGS
- ❏ TUSKS AND LONG TONGUE (EXCEPT FOR MEDUSA)
- ❏ LOOKING AT THEM TURNS YOU INTO STONE

In Poptropica's Mythology Island, you'll encounter Medusa on the way to battle Zeus on Mount Olympus. She is part of a group of three monster sisters known as the Gorgons: Stheno (the Strong One), Euryale (of the Wide Briny Sea), and Medusa (the Queen).

Medusa was the only sister who was part human, and so even though she had snakes for hair, she is often portrayed with a beautiful face.

Some legends say that Athena got angry with Medusa and turned her hair into snakes, which is why Athena's shield has a Gorgon head on it.

Medusa died when the young hero Perseus cut off her head. But even her severed head had the power to turn those who looked on it into stone.

The Gorgons were said to be the daughters of a sea god named Phorcys and his wife, Keto. Together, they produced many frightening sea creatures.

POP FACTS

In the United States, you can find several hair salons named after Medusa.

POP CULTURE

The Minotaur

He Wasn't That Bad, If You Overlook the Whole "Eating People" Thing

- ❑ BODY OF A MAN
- ❑ HEAD OF A BULL
- ❑ LIKED TO EAT PEOPLE

If you can't get through the Minotaur's maze in Mythology Island, the worst thing that will happen is that he won't give you the golden ring in his nose. In the myths, the Minotaur liked to snack on the young men and women who entered his labyrinth.

It was actually King Minos of Crete who kept the Minotaur in a maze. He sacrificed teenagers to the Minotaur until a young hero named Theseus came along and volunteered to enter the labyrinth. The king's daughter, Ariadne, liked Theseus and wanted to help him. She talked to the guy who made the labyrinth,

48

and he told her what to do. She gave Theseus a ball of thread. He went through the maze, unrolling the thread as he went. When he found the Minotaur, he killed him with his bare hands. Then he followed the thread back out of the labyrinth to safety.

He Did What?

YOU MIGHT THINK THESEUS AND ARIADNE GOT MARRIED AFTER THAT, BUT THESEUS EVENTUALLY DUMPED HER ON AN ISLAND. FORTUNATELY, SHE MARRIED THE GOD DIONYSUS AND BECAME IMMORTAL.

MEET THE MINOTAUR

Meet the Heroes

You've probably noticed by now that a lot of the stories about gods and monsters have human (or mostly human) heroes in them. Tales of heroes were very popular in Greek myths.

Heroes usually fit into one or more of these categories:

- Their mother or father is immortal.
- They were separated from their mother or father at birth and need to search for them.
- They are given one or more difficult tasks by a god with a reward promised at the end.
- They face many obstacles along the way.

If you explore Poptropica's Mythology Island, you will discover that *you* are the hero of that adventure, given a series of tasks by Zeus himself. You will definitely face many obstacles before you succeed. But that's the fun part!

BECOME A GOD!

Perseus

A Long Road to a Happy Ending

The famous Greek Perseus had an exciting adventure involving plenty of gods and monsters. Follow the path to join Perseus on his journey.

START

PERSEUS IS BORN TO THE GOD ZEUS AND A PRINCESS NAMED DANAE.

DANAE'S DAD, KING ACRISIUS, IS AFRAID OF A PROPHECY THAT SAYS PERSEUS WILL ONE DAY KILL HIM.

SO HE LOCKS PERSEUS AND HIS MOM IN A CHEST AND DUMPS IT INTO THE SEA.

THEY LAND ON THE ISLAND OF SERIPHUS, AND PERSEUS GROWS UP THERE.

THE KING, POLYDECTES, WANTS TO MARRY DANAE.

POLYDECTES THINKS HE CAN GET RID OF PERSEUS BY SENDING HIM ON A QUEST.

HE TELLS PERSEUS TO GET THE HEAD OF THE GORGON MEDUSA.

PERSEUS ASKS HERMES AND ATHENA FOR HELP.

HE FOLLOWS THEIR ADVICE AND GETS A PAIR OF FLYING SANDALS, HADES'S HELMET OF INVISIBILITY, AND A BAG TO HOLD MEDUSA'S HEAD.

ATHENA GIVES HIM HER SHIELD.

PERSEUS SNEAKS UP ON MEDUSA WHEN SHE'S SLEEPING.

HE USES THE SHIELD TO DEFLECT HER GAZE SO HE WON'T TURN INTO STONE IF HE LOOKS AT HER.

DETOUR! ON THE WAY HOME, HE SEES THE BEAUTIFUL MAIDEN ANDROMEDA CHAINED TO A ROCK.

SUCCESS! HE CUTS OFF MEDUSA'S HEAD.

← DETOUR

A SEA MONSTER IS ABOUT TO EAT HER.

PERSEUS AND ANDROMEDA GET MARRIED.

PERSEUS USES MEDUSA'S HEAD TO TURN THE SEA MONSTER INTO STONE AND SAVE ANDROMEDA.

ANDROMEDA'S UNCLE WON'T LET HER MARRY PERSEUS, SO HE TURNS HIM INTO STONE.

PERSEUS GIVES THE SHIELD AND HEAD TO ATHENA AND STOPS TURNING PEOPLE INTO STONE.

PERSEUS RETURNS THE SANDALS AND HELMET TO HERMES.

KING POLYDECTES STILL WANTS TO MARRY PERSEUS'S MOM AGAINST HER WILL, SO HE TURNS HIM INTO STONE.

PERSEUS GOES BACK TO HIS BIRTHPLACE WITH HIS MOM AND ANDROMEDA AND ACCIDENTALLY KILLS HIS GRANDFATHER.

PERSEUS BRINGS ANDROMEDA TO SERIPHUS.

PERSEUS AND ANDROMEDA MOVE AWAY AND LIVE HAPPILY EVER AFTER.

FINISH

Perseus and Andromeda's daughter gave birth to Hercules, making Perseus the grandfather of Hercules.

POP CULTURE

Hercules

Proof That Being a Hero Isn't All Glory and Fame

POP FACTS

The name of this hero in Greek is actually Herakles. But the Roman Hercules has become more popular, so it was used for the character in Mythology Island.

HERCULES HERE NOW!

Hercules had to kick into hero mode as soon as he was born. His dad was Zeus and his mom was Alcmene, the human daughter of the hero Perseus. Remember, Zeus was married to Hera, and she got superjealous. When Hercules was born, she sent two serpents to kill him in his crib—and he strangled them with his baby hands.

Hera went on to make Hercules's life a living Underworld. She made him go temporarily insane, and he killed his wife and children. He felt terrible, so

he went to the oracle at Delphi and asked what he could do to make up for this horrible deed.

The oracle told him to serve King Eurystheus for twelve years. The king assigned him twelve challenging labors (see the next page), and Hercules completed them all. He went on to get married again, but his happiness didn't last long. His wife, Deianeira, accidentally killed him with poison.

Has-Been Hero?

In Mythology Island, Hercules is imagined as a has-been hero who's out of shape and running a fast-food place. That's pretty tragic, but not really as tragic as some of the other things the hero had to face.

The Twelve Labors of Hercules

Talk about Dirty Jobs!

1. **KILL THE NEMEAN LION**
   This huge lion had skin that couldn't be pierced by any weapon. Hercules wrestled it to death and then skinned it to make himself a cape.

2. **KILL THE HYDRA**
   This giant swamp monster had nine heads. Hercules figured out how to kill it with the help of his nephew, Iolaus.

3. **CAPTURE THE STAG OF ARCADIA**
   This fast, golden-horned deer was sacred to the goddess Artemis. Hercules chased it for a year before the deer tired and he finally caught it.

4. **CAPTURE THE WILD BOAR OF MOUNT ERYMANTHUS**
   Hercules tracked this boar through deep snow and captured it in a net. When he brought it back to Eurystheus, the king was so scared, he jumped into a jar.

5. CLEAN THE STABLES OF AUGEAS IN ONE DAY

King Augeas had an enormous herd of cattle, and their stables were filled with miles of poo. Hercules solved the problem by diverting a river to clean them.

6. SHOOT THE STYMPHALIAN BIRDS

These man-eating birds had sharp feathers that they could shoot like arrows. Hercules used a rattle to make them fly out of the thick grass, and then shot them down with his bow and arrow (or in some stories, a sling).

7. CAPTURE THE CRETAN BULL

Hercules captured this powerful bull pretty easily and brought it back to Eurystheus. Then he let it loose, and it terrorized the countryside. But at least Hercules kept his end of the bargain.

8. CAPTURE THE MAN-EATING MARES OF DIOMEDES

Diomedes was a king who fed his horses human flesh. Hercules fed Diomedes to the horses and then brought them to Eurystheus.

9. TAKE THE BELT OF HIPPOLYTA

Hippolyta was the warrior-queen of the Amazons, and Ares gave her the belt that she wore. Hercules killed her to get the belt.

10. STEAL THE CATTLE OF GERYON

Geryon was a giant with three bodies and four wings who owned an awesome herd of cattle. To steal them, Hercules killed the cowherd, the two-headed guard dog, and finally Geryon.

11. STEAL THE GOLDEN APPLES

The tree of golden apples was guarded by a dragon with one hundred heads, and three nymphs called the Hesperides. Hercules killed the dragon and took the apples—but Athena later returned them.

12. CAPTURE CERBERUS

This three-headed, monstrous dog guarded the Underworld. Hercules took it with the help of Persephone, the wife of Hades.

Atalanta

You Wouldn't Want to Lose a Race to Her

Abandoned in the wilderness by her father when she was born, Atalanta was rescued by bears and then raised by hunters. She grew to become a skilled hunter herself. She became famous during a contest to kill the Calydonian Boar. Atalanta won, and she was given the skin of the boar as a prize. Her uncles tried to take the skin from her, so she killed them.

Probably because she was such an amazing hunter (and beautiful, besides), lots of guys wanted to marry Atalanta. She really wasn't interested, so she said that anyone who could beat her in a footrace could marry her. Lots of guys tried and lost, and Atalanta killed them all.

Then along came a guy named Melanion (or his name might have been Hippomenes). He appealed to the goddess Aphrodite for help, so she gave him three golden apples. During the race, he dropped the apples at different times. Atalanta stopped to pick them up, slowing her down, and Melanion won the race.

The two got married and were pretty happy for a while—until Zeus turned them both into lions.

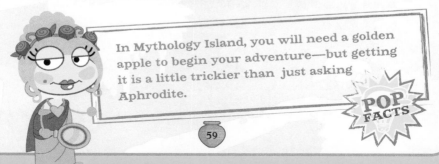

In Mythology Island, you will need a golden apple to begin your adventure—but getting it is a little trickier than just asking Aphrodite.

POP FACTS

Pop Quiz

1. WHICH OF THESE REALMS WOULD YOU RULE, IF YOU COULD?
    A. THE SKY
    B. THE SEA
    C. THE UNDERWORLD

2. WHICH GODDESS WOULD YOU GIVE THE GOLDEN APPLE TO?
    A. HERA
    B. ATHENA
    C. APHRODITE

3. WHAT DO YOU THINK OF HERCULES?
    A. BRAVE HERO
    B. BIG BRUTE
    C. JUST DID WHAT HE NEEDED TO SURVIVE

4. WHICH MAGICAL OBJECT WOULD YOU LIKE TO HAVE?
    A. ZEUS'S THUNDERBOLT
    B. HADES'S HELMET OF INVISIBILITY
    C. HERMES'S WINGED SANDALS

5. IF YOU GOT CURSED BY A GOD, WOULD YOU RATHER . . .
    A. HAVE YOUR HAIR TURNED INTO SNAKES?
    B. BE TURNED INTO A SPIDER?
    C. HAVE THE LOWER BODY OF A HORSE?

6. WHO WOULD WIN IN A FIGHT? CHECK OFF YOUR ANSWER.

❑ CYCLOPS	❑ SPHINX	❑ ATHENA
❑ CENTAUR	❑ HYDRA	❑ APHRODITE
❑ SIRENS	❑ POSEIDON	❑ HERMES
❑ HARPIES	❑ HADES	❑ ARES